Word Wizard

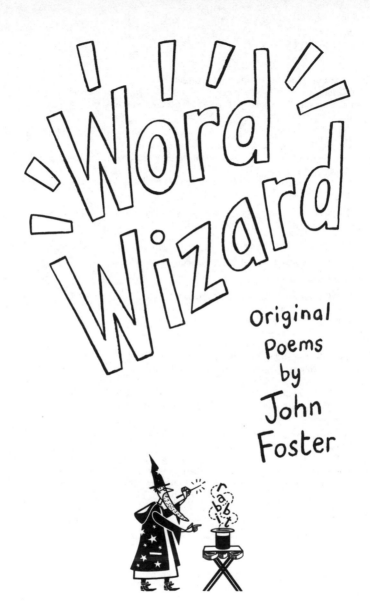

Word Wizard

Original
Poems
by
John
Foster

OXFORD
UNIVERSITY PRESS

OXFORD
UNIVERSITY PRESS

Great Clarendon Street, Oxford OX2 6DP

Oxford University Press is a department of the University of Oxford.
It furthers the University's objective of excellence in research, scholarship,
and education by publishing worldwide in

Oxford New York

Athens Auckland Bangkok Bogotá Buenos Aires
Cape Town Chennai Dar es Salaam Delhi Florence Hong Kong Istanbul
Karachi Kolkata Kuala Lumpur Madrid Melbourne Mexico City Mumbai
Nairobi Paris São Paulo Shanghai Singapore Taipei Tokyo Toronto Warsaw

with associated companies in Berlin Ibadan

Oxford is a registered trade mark of Oxford University Press
in the UK and in certain other countries

British Library Cataloguing in Publication Data available

ISBN 0-19-276270-2

1 3 5 7 9 10 8 6 4 2

Inside illustrations by Ian Whadcock

Designed by StoreyBooks

Typeset by Mary Tudge (Typesetting Services)

Printed in the UK by Cox & Wyman Ltd. Reading, Berkshire

Contents

Poems Are Like People

Poems are like people
Some timid, some bold,
Some hot with passion,
Some icy cold.
Some shout ecstatically,
Some whinge and whine
Some lead you enticingly
   line by line.
Some tease you with a rhyme.

Some dance with skipping feet
Some make your heart
   miss a beat.
Some vex, some inspire.
Some fill you with desire.
Some touch your deepest fears.
Some bring smiles.
     Some bring tears.

Children's Prayer

Let the teachers of our class
Set us tests that we all pass.
Let them never ever care
About what uniform we wear.
Let them always clearly state
It's OK if our homework's late.
Let them say it doesn't matter
When we want to talk and chatter.

Let our teachers shrug and grin
When we make an awful din.
Let them tell us every day
There are no lessons. Go and play.
Let them tell our mum and dad
We're always good and never bad.
Let them write in their report
We are the best class they have taught!

The Schoolkids' Rap

Miss was at the blackboard writing with the chalk,
When suddenly she stopped in the middle of her talk.
She snapped her fingers—snap! snap! snap!
Pay attention children and I'll teach you how to rap.

She picked up a pencil, she started to tap.
All together children, now clap! clap! clap!
Just get the rhythm, just get the beat.
Drum it with your fingers, stamp it with your feet.

That's right, children, keep in time.
Now we've got the rhythm, all we need is the rhyme.
This school is cool. Miss Grace is ace.
Strut your stuff with a smile on your face.

Snap those fingers, tap those toes.
Do it like they do it on the video shows.
Flap it! Slap it! Clap! Snap! Clap!
Let's all do the schoolkids' rap!

Hello, Mr Visitor

Hello, Mr Visitor
Have you come to visit miss?
Are you her boyfriend?
D' you want to give her a kiss?

Are you a parent
Who's come up to complain?
Or are you the plumber
Who's come to fix the drain?

Are you an inspector
Who's come to test our skill?
Is that why the headteacher
Is looking pale and ill?

Are you the dreaded ghost
Of the teacher who said:
'You'll be the death of me!'
And dropped down dead?

Hello, Mr Visitor
Who would you like to see?
Welcome to our school
Whoever you may be!

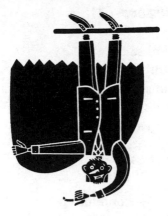

The Friendly Vampire

'Come in,' the friendly vampire said.
'There's room in my tomb for two.
Together we'll have a late-night bite
And I'll share my drink with you!'

      The man shook his head.
      'I'd rather be dead!'
      The vampire gave a grin.
      He took a peck
      At the poor man's neck
      And greedily sucked him in.

The Word Wizard (1)

The Word Wizard said,
'Think of a word.'
What a lot of nonsense!
I thought: *Drivel*.
'To find what urges you to act,'
said the Wizard,
'Subtract the last letter.'
Drive.
'Now, remove the second letter.
Go on. Take the plunge!'
Dive.
'To reveal a contraction,
Cross out the first letter.'
I've.
'Take away the middle letter
And you'll see *that is* an abbreviation.'
i.e.
'Finally, lose the last letter
And find yourself.'
I.

The Word Wizard (2)

The Word Wizard said,
'Take your surname.
It's something to cherish.'
Foster.
Remove the initial letter. Rotate the rest
And find a place to keep your things.
Store.
Tear away the first letter. Go on!
Now look at what you've just done!
Tore.
Carefully pick out the 'r'. But watch your step.
You don't want to tread on one of them!
Toe.
Keep going. Knock off the final letter
And point yourself in the direction you've chosen.
To.
Well done! You're getting the hang of these puzzles.
In fact, if you remove the vowel
You've got this one down to a
T.

The Word Wizard (3)

The Word Wizard said,
'Think of another surname.'
Slater, I thought.
'To find something to put on your roof,
Or that you might like to wipe clean,'
Said the Word Wizard. 'Remove the last letter.'
Slate.
'Now take away the first letter.
Be quick about it or you may not get there in time!'
Late.
'Chop off the first letter
And think about what you did at breakfast-time.'
Ate.
'To discover a word which indicates your location,
Delete the last letter.'
At.
'Finally, lose the consonant
And find the leading vowel in the alphabet.'
A.

SLATER

Some Words

Some words whisper—soft and slow.
Some words shout—thunder, GO!
Some words scamper—patter, leap.
Some words plod—thick, chore, creep.
Some words laugh—jolly, lilt.
Some words scowl—grim and guilt.
Some words tickle—frisky, kiss.
Some words scratch—jab, jeer, hiss.

Wordspinning

Spin pins into nips.
Snap pans into naps.
Mix spit into tips.
Turn parts into traps.

Switch post into stop.
Whisk dear into dare.
Carve hops into shop.
Rip rate into tear.

Twist tame into mate.
Make mean into name.
Juggle taste into state
In the wordspinning game.

A Ragman's Puzzle

Why is a foal like a loaf?
Why is an atom like a moat?
Why is a grin like a ring?
Why is toast like a stoat?

Why is a plum like a lump?
Why is a pager like a grape?
Why is a shrub like a brush?
Why is peat like a tape?

Why are gates like a stage?
Why is a leap like a plea?
Why is a café like a face?
Why is a leaf like a flea?

making amends

as mend   send Ma
Des man   Ma's den
Ned's ma   Sam 'n' Ed
sand me   sad men
a   mends

Mixed Fortunes

soft rune
  stone fur
    foes turn

Exceptional Circumstances

Because the clock was wound up.
Because the saucer won the cup.

Because the polish lost its rag.
Because the roof began to lag.

Because the sky was feeling blue.
Because the meat was in a stew.

Because the ice-cubes lost their cool.
Because the fishes bunked off school.

Because the postman left his post.
Because the ghoul gave up the ghost.

Split Infinitives

to slowly break apart
to carelessly divide
to deliberately separate

to accidentally tear
to cruelly slice
to totally disintegrate

Thin Poems

Thin poems slide down the windowpane of the page like tears, slip under doors leaving messages of farewell then disappear like whispers in the wind.

Concrete Poems

concrete poems
are hard to read
pneumatic
drills
are
what
Y
O
U
N
E
E
D
concrete poems are hard to crack
it's builders who have got the knack

IMPRESSIVE
INDIVIDUAL
INDEPENDENT

I   I   I
N   S   N
S   O   S
U   L   U
L   A   L
A   T   A
R   E   R
     D

ISLAND   I   ISLAND

IMPERIOUS

Staple Diet

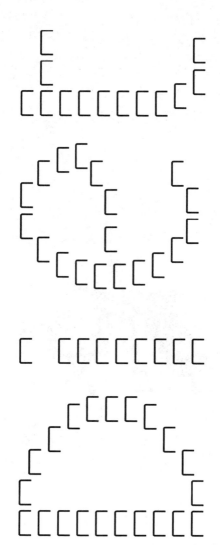

Nothing Ode

O zerO
NOught
NOthing
NOne
O zerO

Word Building (1)

The Word Wizard said:
Start at the very beginning:
A.
Be polite. Place a t in front.
Say thank you!
Ta!
Now for a cuppa!
Drop in an e.
Tea.
To find a friend,
Add in an m and stir.
Mate.
Put an s on one end.
Go on, you choose.
Either lots of friends—
Mates
Or what you need to let off
When you feel you're going to burst—
Steam.
Now insert an r
And get carried away by the flow:
Stream.
Give the letters a good shake
And you'll find out who's in charge:
Master.

Word Building (2)

The Word Wizard said:
Start with nothing:
O.
Add an r if you want an alternative:
Or.
Put a t in front
For a small hill:
Tor.
Then an e behind
To learn things parrot-fashion:
Rote.
Stir in an s
For a place to shop:
Store.
With a y on the end
It'll sound like a tale
But be one of several floors:
Storey.
Put in a d,
Shuffle the pack carefully
And you'll find a verb
That could bring the whole house down:
Destroy.

A cross stick?

A cross stick?
Can't understand what sir's
Rabbiting
On about
So I
Thought
I'd
Compose a poem instead.

Raging Toothache

Throwing a tantrum
Offensive language
Oaths and blasphemies
Terrible temper
Hollering and yelling

How to write cinquains?

I am
counting out the
syllables in each line
to make sure that I've written a
cinquain.

I am
not really sure
that counting syllables
is the best way to make you write
good poems.

By Comparison

Claire's debonaire, but Amanda is grander.
Daisy is lazy but Jean's very keen.
Heidi's untidy, but Margarite's neat.
Bertie is dirty, but Nadine is clean.

Frankie is swanky, but Shaun is withdrawn
Solly is jolly, but Brad's very sad.
Hannah's got manners, but Ruth is uncouth.
Patty is batty and Maddie's quite mad.

Connie is bonny, but Jane's very plain.
Ted is well-bred, but Jude's very crude.
Lester's a jester, but Dave's very grave.
Billy's just silly, but Gertrude is rude!

Living Up To Their Names

Frankie was frantic.
Harriet was harassed.
Anna was anxious.
Emma embarrassed.

Jade was jaded.
Carol was singing.
Stan was standoffish.
Isabel ringing.

Quite Right, Mrs Wright

On the night before the first night of *Twelfth Night*
Dwight Wright had stagefright,
And Mrs Wright said, 'Don't get uptight, Dwight,
It'll be all right on the night.'

On the night after the first night of *Twelfth Night*
Dwight Wright said, 'In spite
Of being uptight with stagefright, it went all right.
You were quite right, Mrs Wright.'

Who'll Go, If You'll Go

Do you know Hugo?
He'll go if I'll go
And Hugh'll go, if you'll go.
So . . . Hugo'll go and Hugh'll go
If I go and you go
That's who'll go, if you'll go.

Just About

Justin Aminute and Justin Case
were going on holiday.
Justin Case packed three cases
And two of everything.
He was ready one hour
Before they were due to leave.
Justin Aminute left it so late
That he couldn't find his suitcase.
He packed in such a hurry
That he left his passport behind
And they only got to the airport
Just in time.

Epitaph: Sandra Slater

Here lies what's left of Sandra Slater
Who poked her pet—an alligator—
Forgetting that to tease or bait her
Might annoy an alligator.

Alas, the alligator ate her.

Epitaph: Percy Thistle

Here lies the body
Of Percy Thistle,
A ref who's blown
His final whistle.

Dead End

In memory of Charlotte Cul-de-sac,
A loyal and trusted friend.
She finally lived up to her name
And came to a dead end.

In Memoriam

Here lies the body
Of Reginald Hacking.

It was his cough
That bore him off.

Knights and Their Habits

Cir Cumference goes round and round.
Sur Vey looks closely at the ground.
Sur Plus is given to excess.
Sur Render yields under duress.
Sur Prise has something else in store.
Sur Charge will make you pay some more.
Sur Pass is greater in extent.
Cir Cus lives in a great big tent.
Sir Loin eats only first-class food.
Sur Ly is bad-tempered and rude.
Sur Face is quite superficial.
Cer Tificate makes it official.

Fun With Puns

I'm really trying

My dad says my report is bad.
He says I must be lying
When I tell him that my teacher
Tells me I'm really trying.

What to do if you have toothache

If your tooth is aching,
Here's what you have to do—
To get rid of the pain, find a window
And stick your head right through!

Question Time

Why are old candles like the Parthenon?
They are both pillars of ancient Greece!
Why is war like a coda?
They both bring an end to a piece!

Hysterical Historicals

Hereward the Wake

Hereward the Wake
Had sleepless nights
Because of his bad back.
He was appropriately named
For an insomniac.

Turning the Tide

After wetting his feet, King Canute is said
To have laughed as he lay in his royal bed.
'I never thought I could control the sea,
But I sure made sure you'd remember me!'

Edward the Confessor

Edward the Confessor
Was a conscientious king.
He felt so guilty appearing in court
He confessed to anything.

William the Conkerer

William the Conqueror's
passion for conkers
is said to have driven
his barons bonkers.

What the King Said to Wat Tyler

You peasants are quite revolting,
Go away and come back in a hour.
We cannot discuss your demands
Until you have all had a shower.

Why Elizabeth I Never Married

She couldn't find a suitor to suit her
Among all her courtiers at court.
As she smoothed down her dress,
She said, 'Well, I guess,
I'm just not the marrying sort.'

We Are Not Amused

The reasons that Queen Victoria
Had frequent bouts of the vapours
Were the stories of royal scandals
She'd read in the tabloid papers.

Neil Armstrong—A Clerihew

Neil Armstrong
Wasn't on the moon for long.
But in that time he left behind
A giant footprint for mankind.

Why the Dinosaurs Became Extinct

The reason for the extinction
Of the whole of the dinosaur race
Is that one day the Earth began spinning so fast
They were all flung off into space.

At King Neptune's Party

At King Neptune's party
The whales had a whale of a time.
The octopus did the eightsome reel
The sea slug slithered in slime.

The sea horse pranced. The dolphins danced.
The seals performed their tricks.
The eels wriggled. The jellyfish giggled.
The snapper took lots of pics.

The mermaids let their hair down.
The sea lion gave a roar.
The porpoise played. The swordfish swayed.
The crabs all waved a claw.

Flying fish did aerobatics.
The turtles did the twist.
Tuna played tunes. Oysters swooned.
Lobsters blushed and kissed.

At King Neptune's party
The whales had a whale of a time.
The octopus did the eightsome reel.
The sea slug slithered in slime.

Sky-Dragon

I am Sky-Dragon,
Lord of the thunder.
When I bellow and roar,
Clouds tear asunder.

When I raise my claw,
The pouring rain
Cascades from the sky
Flooding valley and plain.

When I lash my tail,
The howling gales
Snap the masts of ships
And shred their sails.

When I breathe my fire,
Zigzag stripes
Flash through the sky
As the lightning strikes.

I am Sky-Dragon,
When you hear me roar,
Fasten your windows
And bolt the door!

The Night Before the Match

The night before the match
I lie awake in bed
With thoughts of what might happen
Whirling round my head.

What if there's an open goal
And somehow I fail to score?
What if I miss a penalty
And we lose instead of draw?

What if I miss a tackle
And give a goal away?
What if I get a red card?
What will people say?

What if I'm clean through
And I slip and tread on the ball?
What if I'm ill in the morning
And can't even play at all?

The night before the match
It's always the same.
Why can't I feel like Dad who says:
'Don't worry. It's only a game.'

One to Eleven—Football Speak

'It's a game of two halves,'
said the pundit knowingly.
'And?' I enquired.
'One pitch, three officials,
four goalposts, and two crossbars.
Five penalties, when there's a shoot-out,
And, in the old days, five forwards
And five defenders.
Plus, of course, the goalkeeper,
Which makes six.'
'I see,' I said.
'And I suppose the crowd
Is in seventh heaven
When their team scores.'
'That's right,' said the pundit.
'Number 8 is the inside right,
Or was. Nowadays he could be
Either in midfield or a striker.'
'But number 9's always
The centre forward,' I said.
'Yes, though they'll tell you:
There's only one Alan Shearer.
There's eleven players on each side,
Unless one gets a red card,
Then they're down to ten men.
And the tenth team in the Premiership
Is bottom of the top half.'
'Oh,' I said. 'What about the manager?'
'He's on his own,' said the pundit.
'Unless his team do the double,
Then he's one in a million.'

There's Only One Michael Owen!

Why is it that football commentators
Often refer to players
As though there are several of them?
They go on about
'the likes of your Michael Owens.'
Don't they realize
THERE'S ONLY ONE MICHAEL OWEN!
Have they been watching
so many replays of *that goal*
that they've started to suffer
from double vision?

Immigration Trap

Farida's mum is being sent home.
But Farida's allowed to stay.
Farida doesn't want her to go
But she doesn't have a say.

Farida's lived here all her life.
She's British like you, like me.
But Farida's mum came here
As a stateless refugee.

And now the men who make the rules
Say Farida's mum must go
Back to the land she left
Twelve long years ago.

Back to a troubled land
Where people live in fear.
She has outstayed her welcome.
She is not wanted here.

But because Farida was born here,
Farida's allowed to stay.
She doesn't want her mum to go,
But she doesn't have a say.

How much more?

Downstairs
The raised voices
Reach a crescendo.

The front door slams
Like a pistol shot.

The whole house shudders.

From the living-room
I can hear sobbing.

I huddle under the duvet
And wonder
How much longer it will go on
And how much more
Any of us can take.

Walk Tall

'Walk tall,' Dad said. 'Hold up your head.
Don't ever let them see
You're scared.'

But there are four of them
And only one of me.

As I walk past, they turn and stare,
But I don't let them see
I'm scared,

'Cause there are four of them
And only one of me.

Part of the Deal

They said it was part of the deal,
If I wanted to join the gang,
So I joined in the jeering and sneering
When they picked on Tony Chang.

I was there when they let down his tyres.
I was there when they tore his shirt.
I was there when they emptied his satchel
And trampled his books in the dirt.

They said it was part of the deal
And I wanted to join the gang.
But now I'm ashamed that I joined in
When they picked on Tony Chang.

Empty Canvas

They have stolen
The colours from my paintbox.
I have only
Brown for the splinters of shrapnel,
Grey for the widow's ashen face,
White for the winding shroud.
My canvas is empty
Save for the streaks of my tears.

Just In Case

'You never know what's around the next corner,'
said Grandad.
'Which is why you should hedge your bets
And never give up the unequal struggle.'

Even in his eighties,
He kept on doing his allotment,
Planting two rows of everything,
'Just in case.'

Definition: Potatoes

Ordinary fellows
Dressed in brown jackets.
Sons of the soil,
White as British holidaymakers
When relieved of their skins,
But crisp, golden brown when fried:
Chips off the old block—
Except when blighted.

All Things Dry and Dusty

All things dry and dusty,
All plants shrivelled and small,
All trees bare and blighted,
It's man who made them all.

The shoots that twist and wither,
The rotten leaves that fall,
The fruits that do not ripen,
It's man who made them all.

All things dry and dusty,
All plants shrivelled and small,
All trees bare and blighted,
It's man who made them all.

The fields that yield no harvest,
The empty market stall,
The orchard's fruitless trees,
It's man who made them all.

All things dry and dusty,
All plants shrivelled and small,
All trees bare and blighted,
It's man who made them all.

The Wild Wind

Sweeping down the street,
Swerving through the trees,
Snatching leaves and twigs
To whisk in its breeze.

Whistling round the chimneys,
Whooshing under floors,
Sniffing at the windows,
Snapping shut the doors.

Shattering the silence
Wherever it goes,
Swirling, twirling, whirling,
The wild wind blows.

Autumn News Bulletin

Today, the trees are in shock.
Overnight, a sustained assault
Has left them battered and bare.
There are leaves everywhere—
On roads and pathways,
Scattered on lawns and flowerbeds,
Clustered in doorways
And the corners of buildings.

In some gardens
Men with rakes have appeared.
In due course, barrow loads of leaves
Will be heaped into bonfires.
Now, in the aftermath of the storm,
There is an air of resignation.
As one of the residents put it:
'I suppose it's to be expected.
It happens every year.'

Spring Haiku

Pale lemon primroses
Whispering promises of summer
On a dull March day.

Swaying in the breeze,
Their heads nodding, bluebells ring,
Heralding summer.

Golden daffodils
Trumpeting triumphantly
Proclaim: Spring is here!

Haiku

Bright as butterflies
With folded wings, the windsurfs
Skim across the bay.

Grey as steel, the sea
Shimmers in the fading light:
Day slides into night.

Blackbird

Blackbird
Hops, stops, hops, stops,
Across the lawn. Listens,
Its head cocked for sounds of a worm,
Then strikes.

Listen! Can You Hear . . .

the whispering wings of a butterfly
the shimmering petal's gentle sigh
the fluttering clouds slipping by

the glimmering glow of the sun's bright beam
the muttering murmur of a shaded stream
the fleeing footprints of a dream.

At the Gate

Thoughtful,
The old man stands,
Resting against the gate,
Wondering when it will open,
Waiting.

This Poem Is Shy

This poem is shy.
It does not crave the spotlight.
It prefers to sit in silence,
Watching, waiting in the wings,
For someone to glance in its direction.
When it meets the eye,
It smiles,
Rekindling memories
Of the scent of roses
And the soft touch of summer breezes,
Before slipping back
To rest upon the page
Patiently.